# The Lonesome Boy and the Blonde Haired Angel

## Written by Alex Fischetti

## Illustrated by Cleveland Miller

Dedicated to my buddy Reeny who opened my eyes to all that is good in the world. ~ A.F.

This book is dedicated to all the special angels who lift up the spirits and lives of those around them. Just like my dear friend Alex, and his dear friend Reeny, who were the inspiration for this story. And to my two loving children, Matthew and Andrew. May you be blessed in the Lord forever. ~ C.M.

This young man is Ernie. On the outside he looks like any other average human being.

He talks, he walks, and he does the normal things just like most human beings do. But there is something different about him. At a young age Ernie was diagnosed with Asperger Syndrome.

Asperger Syndrome is a form of Autism which affects how people think and socialize.

People who have Aspergers don't necessarily understand how to interact with other people like regular human beings do.

It was a very sad reality for Ernie.

Jeremiah 1:5 Jeremiah 1:5: "Before I formed you in the womb I knew you, and before you were born I consecrated you; I have appointed you a prophet to the nations.

Psalm: 25:16 Turn to me and be gracious to me, for I am lonely and afflicted.

Ernie had trouble finding friends.

Anytime he would meet someone close to his age there was always something about him that made the person think he was weird.

Because of that, hardly anyone wanted to be around him.

Poor Ernie was always by himself.
All during school time, Ernie was alone.
At a cafeteria lunch table, at the playground, everywhere.

There never seemed to be the right person for him to be around.

Isaiah: 41:10 So do not fear, for I am with you; do not be dismayed, for I am your God. I will strengthen you and help you; I will uphold you with my righteous right hand.

1 Samuel 12:22 For the sake of his great name the Lord will not reject his people, because the Lord was pleased to make you his own.

Moving from place to place didn't help much either.

Ernie's dad had a job that required traveling and one day he announced that the family will be moving to Florida.

So Ernie and his family packed up the house, said goodbye to Connecticut where they lived at the time and off they went.

Deuteronomy: 31:6 Be strong and courageous. Do not be afraid or terrified because of them, for the Lord your God goes with you; he will never leave you nor forsake you.

1 Samuel 12:22 For the sake of his great name the Lord will not reject his people, because the Lord was pleased to make you his own.

In Florida, when Ernie had free time while not in school, he always went to the library. It never ceased to amaze the librarians how he could read something so many times and never get bored!

Despite all this, Ernie still felt sad because he was lonely, so he decided to pray about it.

No matter what he went through as a human being with Aspergers, God was always there for him.

But now he felt he needed the Lord's help more than ever.

He prayed for The Lord to ease the pain he still had in his heart.

Philippians: 4:6 Do not be anxious about anything, but in every situation, by prayer and petition, with thanksgiving, present your requests to God.

The Lord always is hard at work for his sons and daughters.

The night Ernie prayed that prayer, I guess you can say heaven was on fire.

Now God gives us blessings that just blow our minds.

And Ernie was about to be blessed BIG TIME!

The next day began like any other day for our young friend. Ernie went to school and afterwards as he usually did he went to the library to relax after what was a VERY busy day.

Psalm 145:18 The Lord is near to all who call on him, to all who call on him in truth.

James: 1:2-4 1:2-4: Consider it pure joy, my brothers and sisters, whenever you face trials of many kinds, because you know that the testing of your faith produces perseverance. Let perseverance finish its work so that you may be mature and complete, not lacking anything.

As he was walking around looking for a good book to read, he suddenly stopped cold.

Someone sitting at one of the tables caught his attention

It was a woman. She had gorgeous blond hair and she had a smile that made the whole library smile with her.

When the woman saw Ernie, she put out her hand to shake his.

"Hello," she said. "I'm Madeline."

"Hi," said Ernie. "My name is Ernie."

"It's a pleasure to meet you Ernie," said Madeline.

Proverbs: 20:27 The human spirit is the lamp of the LORD that sheds light on one's inmost being.

Matthew: 18:20 For where two or three gathers in my name, there am I with them.

Then Madeline saw the look in Ernie's face and it made her concerned.

"Are you ok?" asked Madeline "You seem upset."
"I apologize." said Ernie, "It was a long day at school."
"Come sit down with me," said Madeline as she pulled up a chair. "Talk to me about what's bothering you."

So, Ernie sat with her and they began a long conversation. Not only did he talk to her about that day's troubles, he went into full detail about his struggles with Aspergers. In return Madeline told Ernie her own trials of being the wife of a Pastor, raising four grown-up kids and being a preschool teacher. Ernie was clearly taken aback by how there was nothing she saw in him that she thought was weird, which seemed rare in his mind.

Hebrews: 10:24-25 And let us consider how we may spur one another on toward love and good deeds, not giving up meeting together, as some are in the habit of doing, but encouraging one another—and all the more as you see the Day approaching.

At Sunday service at church, Ernie saw Madeline and decided he wanted to say thank you for being so nice to him.

When Madeline saw Ernie approach her, she grinned from ear to ear.

"Ernie!" she said, "So great to see you!"

She then wrapped her arms around him and gave him a big hug.

This simple gesture of kindness was something that really touched him.

It was the beginning of a beautiful friendship.

Colossians: 3:14 And over all these virtues put on love, which binds them all together in perfect unity.

One thing about Madeline that Ernie loved the most was how positive she was.

He once said to Madeline that he didn't consider himself to be a good writer.

Madeline responded: "You're a great writer. You just don't give yourself enough credit." After that, Ernie felt more confident in his writing as he started to believe more in his abilities.

Proverbs: 3:5-6 Trust in the Lord with all your heart and lean not on your own understanding; in all your ways submit to him, and he will make your paths straight.

Since Ernie struggled with Aspergers, he found comfort in talking with Madeline about it. He explained to her that ever since he was a kid, it was never easy for him to make friends.

Madeline said: "Don't be afraid to make new friendships and allow others to see you for who you truly are. They will love you, and those who don't aren't worth your time anyway."

Her kind words helped Ernie to reach out to more people, and today he has more friends than he EVER imagined possible.

Proverbs: 13:20 Walk with the wise and become wise, for a companion of fools suffers harm.

Both being Christians, God was always a vocal point of discussion. Every now and again Ernie would have anxiety about waiting for something great to happen to him for his future.

Madeline softly smiled and said: "Calm yourself and take the time to look and see what the Lord has given you." These days Ernie is more thankful for the blessings he receives every day.

Matthew: 6:25-34 Therefore I tell you, do not worry about your life, what you will eat or drink; or about your body, what you will wear. Is not life more than food, and the body more than clothes? Look at the birds of the air; they do not sow or reap or store away in barns, and yet your heavenly Father feeds them. Are you not much more valuable than they? Can any one of you by worrying add a single hour to your life? And why do you worry about clothes? See how the flowers of the field grow. They do not labor or spin. Yet I tell you that not even Solomon in all his splendor was dressed like one of these. If that is how God clothes the grass of the field, which is here today, and tomorrow is thrown into the fire, will he not much more clothe you—you of little faith? So, do not worry, saying, 'What shall we eat?' or 'What shall we drink?' or 'What shall we wear?' For the pagans run after all these things, and your heavenly Father knows that you need them. But seek first his kingdom and his righteousness, and all these things will be given to you as well. Therefore, do not worry about tomorrow, for tomorrow will worry about itself. Each day has enough trouble of its own.

Even though Madeline was a blessed individual, she herself went through her own trials.

Madeline expressed to Ernie that "With God's strength, I always pull through. Only God can make beauty from the ashes."

Her God-given strength was something Ernie had heard and read about, but had never seen in person.

Philippians: 4:13  I can do all this through Christ who gives me strength.

All these AMAZING qualities made Madeline a person Ernie tried to model himself after and made him finally happy about living in FL.

From Madeline's influence, Ernie taught himself to not be quick to judge others, have more patience in difficult situations, and to ALWAYS put on a happy face so that someone's sad day might have a little more light in it.

Galatians: 5:22-26 But the fruit of the Spirit is love, joy, peace, forbearance, kindness, goodness, faithfulness, gentleness and self-control. Against these things there is no law. Those who belong to Christ Jesus have crucified the flesh with its passions and desires. Since we live by the Spirit, let us keep in step with the Spirit. Let us not become conceited, provoking and envying each other.

Unfortunately, because of his dad's job, Ernie had to move back to Connecticut and with that leave Madeline behind.

On their last get together, Ernie gave her a huge hug and told her how he had been crying a lot at the thought of being apart from his hero.

At the end of their meeting, Madeline put her arm around Ernie and gave him these parting words: "Allow yourself to feel those emotions but don't get stuck in them. Feelings will lie to us all the time."

Ernie to this day is still using those words of wisdom to influence his life in a positive way.

Jeremiah 29:11 "For I know the plans I have for you," declares the Lord, "plans to prosper you and not to harm you, plans to give you hope and a future."

Genesis: 2:18 The Lord God said, "It is not good for the man to be alone. I will make a helper suitable for him."

Today if you knew Ernie from his childhood and ran into him today, you would see a great change in him.

Madeline gave Ernie a sense of true friendship and inspiration he had always longed for when he was a child and because of that, he was blessed in the most amazing ways that helped make him into the man that EVERYONE looks up too to this day.

Ernie is here in this photograph somewhere, surrounded by many of his friends.

**Can you find him?**

## There he is!

Right up front!

The people in this picture are just HALF the people he knows!

Ernie knows so many that he is nicknamed The Mayor!
Is God awesome or what?!

Because of one person's kindness, encouragement and love, he has transformed from the Lonesome Boy to the Social Butterfly!

And just like that special angel was there for Ernie, there's one waiting for you too.


Ephesians: 4:29 Do not let any unwholesome talk come out of your mouths, but only what is helpful for building others up according to their needs, that it may benefit those whose listen.

### Top Ten Ways You Can Be A Great Friends To A Person With Aspergers or Autism

1. Be as positive as you can.

2. Have a good sense of humor.

3. Be as patient as possible. Lend a hand when you can see they are struggling.

4. Try not to be judgmental with them.

5. When asking their help for anything, be as SPECIFIC as you possibly can, with what you want them to do, so they can help you without confusion or difficulty.

6. If at any point in the middle of talking to you they suddenly stop to gather their thoughts, give them time. They are trying to find a way to say the right words to say to you without sounding confusing or rude.

7. If you don't know them but frequently see them around town, work, or school, gently ask them to join their circle. If they say yes great, but if they say no, let them have their space.

8. Never FORCE them to do anything. Let them make as many decisions on their own as possible.

9. Take time to learn what makes them happy and what they enjoy doing so you can figure them out better and they in return can be more comfortable with you.

10. Never stop telling them what a blessing they are to you and to the world!

# The Real Ernie and Madeline: Alex and Reeny

## About the real Ernie: Alex Fischetti

Alex Fischetti is an Italian American Christian who tries to be as big a blessing to his family and friends who are blessings to him! He is a writer of books and local news articles and is an usher at the Ridgefield Playhouse. He LOVES going out to lunch with friends, walking around town and traveling to different parts of the east coast particularly in his home state of Connecticut and his birth state of New York.

## About the Illustrator:

Cleveland (Cleo) Miller is a mother to two wonderfully funny, bright and happy boys. She lives in Old Greenwich, CT and loves to go for walks at the beach, forests, and parks. She has been painting and creating art since childhood, loves to sing and dance, and listen to music of all kinds. She considers herself very blessed to have Alex Fischetti as a friend.

## Acknowledgements

With deep gratitude and appreciation, we would like to thank everyone who contributed their talents, efforts, and encouragement to help make this book possible.

Photo Credit on Pages 32 and 34, to Scott Vincent, https://ScottVincentPhoto.com

Location courtesy of The Ridgefield Playhouse, Ridgefield, CT

Photo Credit on Page 40, to Kristen Jensen, https://KristenJensen.com

Special thanks to Lori Berisford, Steve Carlson, Elaine Cox, Kerry Anne Ducey, Don Fertman, Hannah Fischer, Diane Fischetti, Anmarie Galowski, Steve Mignogna, and Lindsey Roth for their generous support, and steadfast enthusiasm.

Made in the USA
Middletown, DE
01 July 2018